Have a question about how you can better leverage technology for your business needs? Email your question to hello@temple.rocks, and write in the subject line: "Marketing Technology Question." In addition to a personal answer, I will send you a FREE copy of the "5 Checks" checklist, where you can see exactly what questions to ask to move your project to the next level. To learn more, visit https://temple.rocks/go/5checks

5 Checks of Working with a Marketing CTO

Factors to Check Before Deploying Ideas

Nick Temple

Foreword by
Mitchell Levy

THiNK*aha*®

An Actionable Business Journal

E-mail: info@thinkaha.com
20660 Stevens Creek Blvd., Suite 210
Cupertino, CA 95014

Published by THiNKaha®
20660 Stevens Creek Blvd., Suite 210, Cupertino, CA 95014
http://thinkaha.com
E-mail: info@thinkaha.com

First Printing: February 2019
Hardcover ISBN: 978-1-61699-311-5   1-61699-311-1
Paperback ISBN: 978-1-61699-310-8   1-61699-310-3
eBook ISBN: 978-1-61699-309-2   1-61699-309-X
Place of Publication: Silicon Valley, California, USA
Paperback Library of Congress Number: 2018914583

Trademarks

Warning and Disclaimer

Acknowledgement

This book is about marketing and technology, so I'd like to say "thank you" to some of the people who showed me the way.

The late Mark Hendricks, whose mentorship and friendship was deeply treasured and who brought compassion and integrity to all his work.

Mark Joyner, the "Godfather of Internet Marketing" and developer of some of the first online marketing tools. Thank you.

Stephanie Frank, who is one of those few souls who gets both sides of the space and has always had an ear when I needed something.

Mike Merz Sr., may the joint ventures abound!

Thank you, Jeffery Martin and Nichol Bradford, for showing me that technology can indeed be used for well-being at a time when I had lost much of my faith in the industry.

Richard Fetik and Mike Graves, you were both instrumental in my early professional technology career—thank you each for your support and the knowledge that you passed on.

Veronica Robinson, thank you for always sticking to the projects, no matter what.

And a special thanks to Ania Krol, Malissa Sullivan, Jenilee Maniti, and Mitchell Levy and team for putting this book together—and your patience. Without you, it simply would not have been possible. Thank you.

Dedication

For Malissa, fast Mustangs, and cross-country trips. May the journey
never end!

How to Read a THiNKaha® Book

A Note from the Publisher

The AHAthat/THiNKaha series is the CliffsNotes of the 21st century. These books are contextual in nature. Although the actual words won't change, their meaning will every time you read one as your context will change. Be ready, you will experience your own AHA moments as you read the AHA messages™ in this book. They are designed to be stand-alone actionable messages that will help you think about a project you're working on, an event, a sales deal, a personal issue, etc. differently. As you read this book, please think about the following:

1. It should only take 15–20 minutes to read this book the first time out. When you're reading, write in the underlined area one to three action items that resonate with you.
2. Mark your calendar to re-read this book again in 30 days.
3. Repeat step #1 and mark one to three more AHA messages that resonate. They will most likely be different than the first time. BTW: this is also a great time to reflect on the AHAmessages that resonated with you during your last reading.

After reading a THiNKaha book, marking your AHA messages, re-reading it, and marking more AHA messages, you'll begin to see how these books contextually apply to you. AHAthat/THiNKaha books advocate for continuous, lifelong learning. They will help you transform your AHAs into actionable items with tangible results until you no longer have to say AHA to these moments—they'll become part of your daily practice as you continue to grow and learn.

Mitchell Levy, The AHA Guy at AHAthat
publisher@thinkaha.com

THiNKaha®

Contents

.

Foreword

Anyone who has worked in business for any length of time has discovered that there are (at least) two different ways of looking at each product: through a marketing, business-centric view and a technological, best practices, elegant view.

So many times, these views butt heads, and it is the rare individual who has the capability to balance the requirements of marketing: customer satisfaction, fast turnaround, and inexpensive implementation with those of technologists—clean code, elegant design, and rock-solid performance.

I met Nick at a marketing conference in 2017, and it quickly became apparent that he is one of those rare individuals who can see both sides: the need for maintainable systems coupled with the business requirements to launch.

When running a business, the CEO should be spending their time marketing and selling their product/service, not building them. While focusing on the needs of the existing and new clients, every CEO could use a Marketing CTO, an individual who can discuss the pluses and minuses, the time to market vs. cost of deployment, and the short-term vs. long-term implications types of questions that allow the CEO's idea to get to the market in a quick and efficient way for today, while having scalability built into the design and maintenance for the long term. When thinking about your next business idea, ask yourself, "Do I have a Marketing CTO I can turn to?"

I'm happy to have helped bring this book together and to bring you *5 Checks of Working with a Marketing CTO.*

Mitchell Levy, The AHA Guy

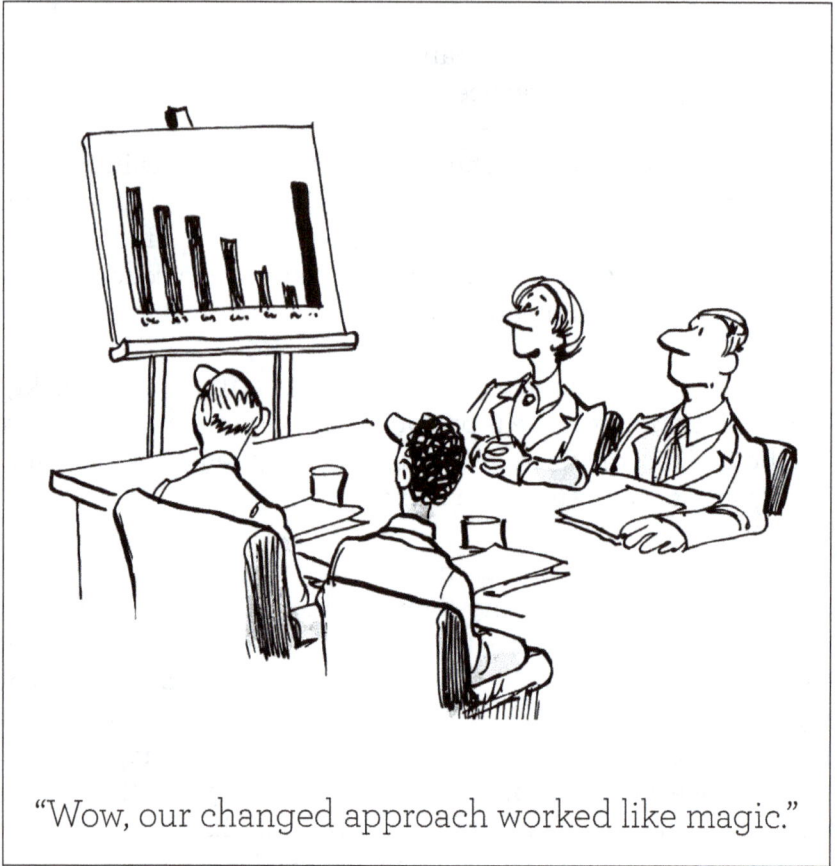

"Wow, our changed approach worked like magic."

Share the AHA messages from this book socially by going to
http://aha.pub/5Checks

Section I

Growing Your Business

Growing a business and making it successful can be a difficult yet rewarding endeavor. What does it take to make your business grow? What do you need to be successful? You must have the proper mindset, attitude, knowledge, and tools to help you and your team scale the business while maintaining its integrity. We all have many ideas every day—which ones will make an impact on the bottom line?

Watch this video: http://aha.pub/5ChecksS1

1

There's a trade-off between doing it "right" and "good enough." Is it good enough to ship? #MarketingCTO

_____

_____

_____

2

Help the people you work with be the best that they can be. Have you adopted this motto yet? #MarketingCTO

_____

_____

_____

3

Core principles of success include being open and honest. That means sometimes delivering bad news. #MarketingCTO

_____

_____

_____

4

How do you grow your business? Find the key leading metrics and focus on them. #MarketingCTO

_____

_____

_____

5

Find someone on the outside who'll give you honest feedback and has no vested interest in selling you something. #MarketingCTO

_____

_____

_____

6

You grow your business by creating appropriate metrics around revenue and customer engagement. #MarketingCTO

_____

_____

_____

7

Don't spend all your resources in making something that looks good but doesn't engage your customers. #MarketingCTO

_____

_____

_____

8

Focus: Follow the 80/20 rule, and reach the 20% of customers who are going to make an impact. #MarketingCTO

_____

_____

_____

9

What makes your business unique?
What makes you different? #MarketingCTO

_____

_____

_____

10

If you're an entrepreneur with many ideas, do the 20% of the work that will get you 80% of the value. #MarketingCTO

_____

_____

_____

11

Get your product out there as quickly as possible, and then figure out where to go from there. #MarketingCTO

_____

_____

_____

12

Streamline and put processes in place so when there's development to be done, it's done in a testable way. #MarketingCTO

_____

_____

_____

13

Ask yourself, "How does this align with what I'm trying to do long term?" #MarketingCTO

_____

_____

_____

14

Successful people complete small projects that are in alignment with their bigger goal. #MarketingCTO

_____

_____

_____

15

Have project lists, like "Active Projects," "Maybe Laters," and "Parking Lot." Review often. #MarketingCTO

_____

_____

_____

16

If you do projects that don't align with your larger goals, you'll end up spreading yourself too thin. #MarketingCTO

_____

_____

_____

17

Revenue is an indicator of positive exchange. Are you providing value to your customers? #MarketingCTO

_____

_____

_____

Share the AHA messages from this book socially by going to
http://aha.pub/5Checks

Section II

Validating Ideas

Business people have many ideas going through their mind. Some may lead to something big, and some may not lead to anything at all. This is why we need to validate the ideas we have. We need to test them to find out which are worth looking at and pursuing. Knowing this will help us save time and money.

Watch this video: http://aha.pub/5ChecksS2

18

It's not only about getting things done but also getting the right things done. #MarketingCTO

_____

_____

_____

19

Start with the smallest thing you can do that will possibly work, before attempting top scale. #MarketingCTO

_____

_____

_____

20

Does it make sense to put together a small project to validate and scale the idea? #MarketingCTO

_____

_____

_____

21

Is this idea time sensitive? If so, then it may be time to move on it now. #MarketingCTO

_____

_____

_____

22

It's possible to get 10 paying customers
with little effort in the initial experiment.
#MakeSense #MarketingCTO

_____

_____

_____

23

The goal of experimentation is to get the
core concepts of the idea and ensure that
there is a market. #MarketingCTO

_____

_____

_____

24

After experimenting with your idea, decide whether to move forward based on technology costs, user interest, and revenue. #MarketingCTO

_____

_____

_____

25

Look at everything on your plate, and ask if this is something you should work on right now. #MarketingCTO

_____

_____

_____

26

After experimenting with your idea, decide whether to continue depending on technology costs, user interest, and revenue. #MarketingCTO

_____

_____

_____

27

Before committing, test your solution
in the marketplace before putting
significant resources into development.
#MarketingCTO

_____

_____

_____

28

With your project, you need to do a gut
check and ask yourself, "Is this the direction
we want to go?" #MarketingCTO

_____

_____

_____

29

You don't need to be perfect. Just get something out there that you can share and see if people are going to buy. #MarketingCTO

_____

_____

_____

30

Validate your idea by getting 10 initial paying customers using minimal investment in technology. #MarketingCTO

_____

_____

_____

31

If you put less effort into failed projects at the beginning, you can usually succeed by pivoting. #MarketingCTO

_____

_____

_____

32

When great ideas are given too many resources at the beginning, they can miss the market with no room to pivot. #MarketingCTO

_____

_____

_____

33

What's the smallest amount of work we can do to get this idea out there and make sure it works? #MarketingCTO

_____

_____

_____

34

Throw your ideas over a wall, have someone look at them critically, then figure out how you can test them.
#MarketingCTO

_____

_____

_____

35

When prototyping, code quality doesn't matter, as long as it does what it must to move the mission forward. #MarketingCTO

_____

_____

_____

36

Use your resources in a way that you're testing the concepts of your ideas. #MarketingCTO

_____

_____

_____

37

Don't immediately engage a large team to build something just because you have a "great" idea. Test first. #MarketingCTO

_____

_____

_____

38

What's the smallest thing you can build that will get you 10 paying customers, even if you have to do it manually? #MarketingCTO

_____

_____

_____

39

How does your product idea fit in with your bigger vision? Are you staying on track? #MarketingCTO

_____

_____

_____

40

Once you know that 10 people are going to buy your product, you'll know that you've got something worth working on. #MarketingCTO

_____

_____

_____

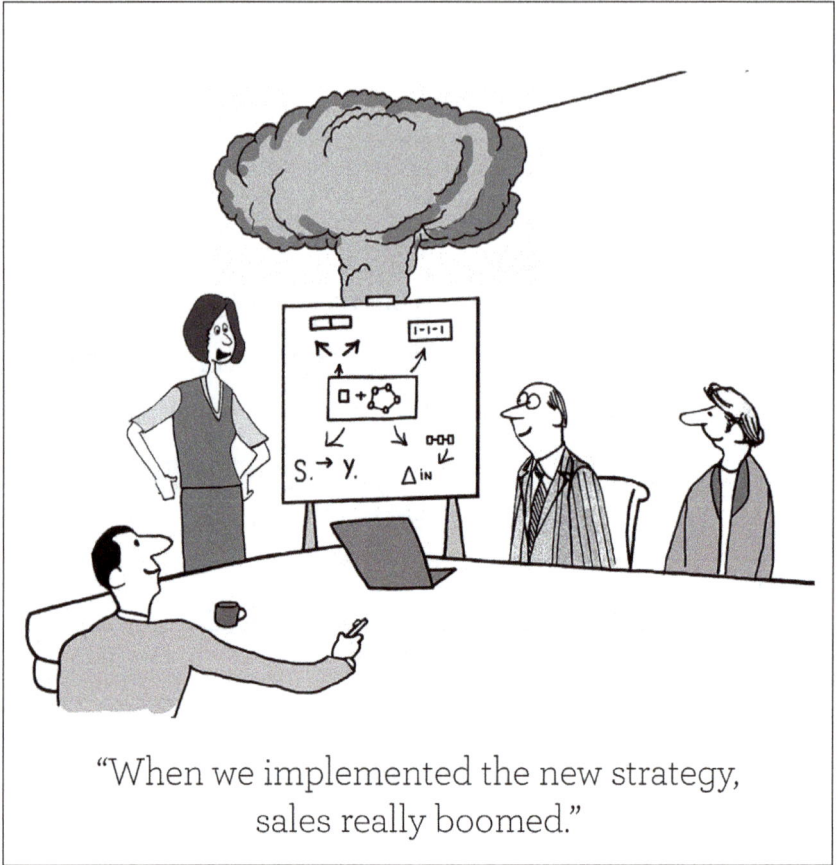

"When we implemented the new strategy, sales really boomed."

Share the AHA messages from this book socially by going to
http://aha.pub/5Checks

Section III

Sanity Check

Although our ideas are promising, not every project is something we want to start today. We have a lot on our plates, and unless you have unlimited time and funding, you need to double check to see if a project is a good idea. Is this the right thing to do, given the other things we have going on? Is it aligned with our current project? It's important to capture and keep track of our ideas so when everything is in alignment, we can get the go-ahead for a project. Does this idea make sense in the marketplace today, given our other commitments?

Watch this video: http://aha.pub/5ChecksS3

41

The stars have to align for a project to get the go-ahead. Is everything in alignment? #MarketingCTO

_____

_____

_____

42

Keep a list of your ideas; prioritize. Which one makes sense to move on today? #MarketingCTO

_____

_____

_____

43

Put your ideas in a parking lot so they're documented and easily available when you need them. #MarketingCTO

_____

_____

_____

44

Capture your ideas and review weekly to see which you should resurrect from the parking lot. #MarketingCTO

_____

_____

_____

45

Go through your captured ideas to
see which you can take off the list and
implement. #MarketingCTO

_____

_____

_____

46

What's the smallest part of a product we
can deploy? What experiment can we do
to see if we want to invest more in an idea?
#MarketingCTO

_____

_____

_____

47

If we can come up with something that's not going to take much time or energy, it makes sense to move on it. #MarketingCTO

_____

_____

_____

48

If the experiment is going to require more resources than you have right now, it would be best to move the idea aside. #MarketingCTO

_____

_____

_____

49

If the idea is not aligned with current goals, move it aside and save it for another time. #MarketingCTO

_____

_____

_____

50

If the idea seems worth pursuing, come up with an inexpensive experiment to validate it. #MarketingCTO

_____

_____

_____

51

You want the ideas you go with to fit within the boundaries of time and other constraints. Are they? #MarketingCTO

_____

_____

_____

52

If we have an idea in alignment with what we're doing, we need to figure out what experiment we can do to test it. #MarketingCTO

_____

_____

_____

53

Look at the resources around your experiment and ask, "Okay, can we move on it?" #MarketingCTO

_____

_____

_____

54

You should keep track of the ideas out there, as well as the current state of technology and the marketplace. #MarketingCTO

_____

_____

_____

55

When new technology comes in that allows your idea to be something worth looking at, take it out of the parking lot. #MarketingCTO

_____

_____

_____

56

Is the idea too small that it doesn't excite you? Is the idea so big that it scares you? What's your idea? #MarketingCTO

_____

_____

_____

57

Most entrepreneurs have more ideas and things to do than they actually have time and resources to get done. Is that you? #MarketingCTO

_____

_____

_____

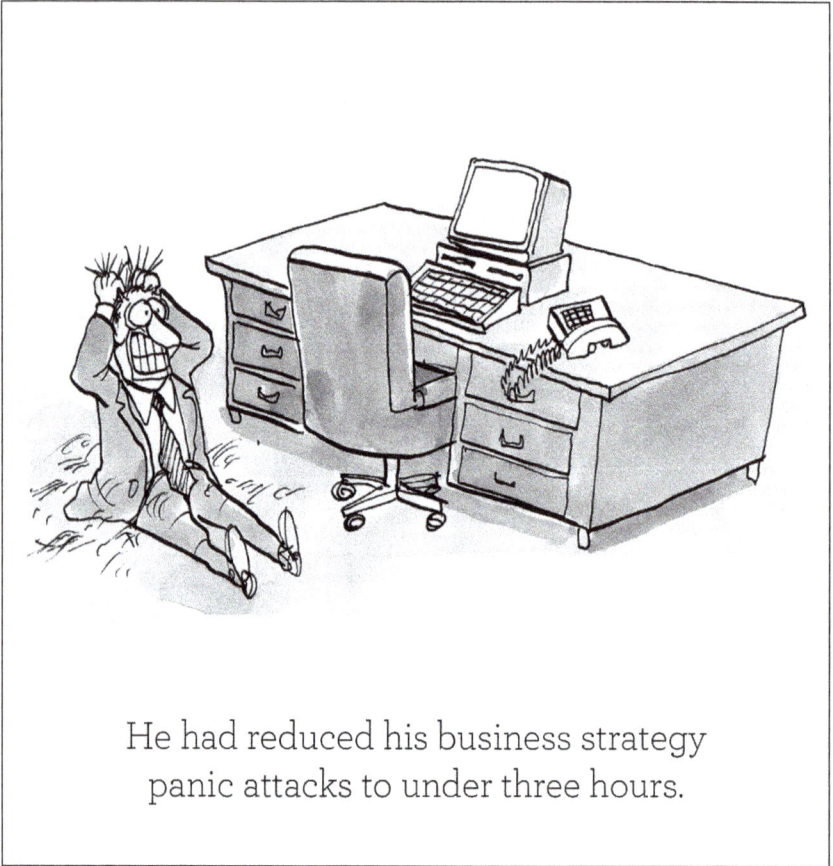

He had reduced his business strategy
panic attacks to under three hours.

Share the AHA messages from this book socially by going to
http://aha.pub/5Checks

Section IV

Resource Check

Before starting another project, we need to ensure that we have the necessary resources for it. If you don't have these available, you won't be able to complete the project and your solution will not reach its full potential. What should you evaluate to see if you have enough resources for a specific project? How can you make the most of your resources?

Watch this video: http://aha.pub/5ChecksS4

58

Before you add anything more to what you're doing, have an inventory of the commitments you currently have. #MarketingCTO

59

Test a big idea by outsourcing a small piece. If it succeeds, then you can take it to the next level. #MarketingCTO

60

Outsourcing can help you get the ball
rolling on an experiment.
Have you tried it? #MarketingCTO

_____

_____

_____

61

If your outsourced experiment comes out
well, then awesome; otherwise, you haven't
lost much time or money. #MarketingCTO

_____

_____

_____

62

Are there resources that can be acquired for a small amount of money that will allow you to leverage what you do? #MarketingCTO

_____

_____

_____

63

Before you start, look at the market timing, your resources, and what you've already got on your plate. #MarketingCTO

_____

_____

_____

64

Are you using all the resources, technology, people, and money you have available? #MarketingCTO

_____

_____

_____

65

What's your time worth? Estimate how much money you're making per day based on your revenue and expenses. #MarketingCTO

_____

_____

_____

66

If an idea becomes a project that you must manage, it will compete for resources with other projects you have. #MarketingCTO

_____

_____

_____

67

You have to think ahead. Does this project lead to something that is so big, only Google could pull it off? #MarketingCTO

_____

_____

_____

68

Free yourself to focus on what you are best
at by pinpointing the things you don't like
doing, and outsourcing. #MarketingCTO

_____

_____

_____

69

Find ways to stay in your lane, and focus on being good at what you want. Do what you love and love what you do. #MarketingCTO

70

Don't outsource the highlight of your day just because you can get somebody else to do it. #MarketingCTO

71

Do you really enjoy doing this specific task? If the answer is yes and it's energizing for you, then keep it. #MarketingCTO

_____

_____

_____

72

Given the resources you have available, what's the best use for your time in terms of making this a successful project? #MarketingCTO

_____

_____

_____

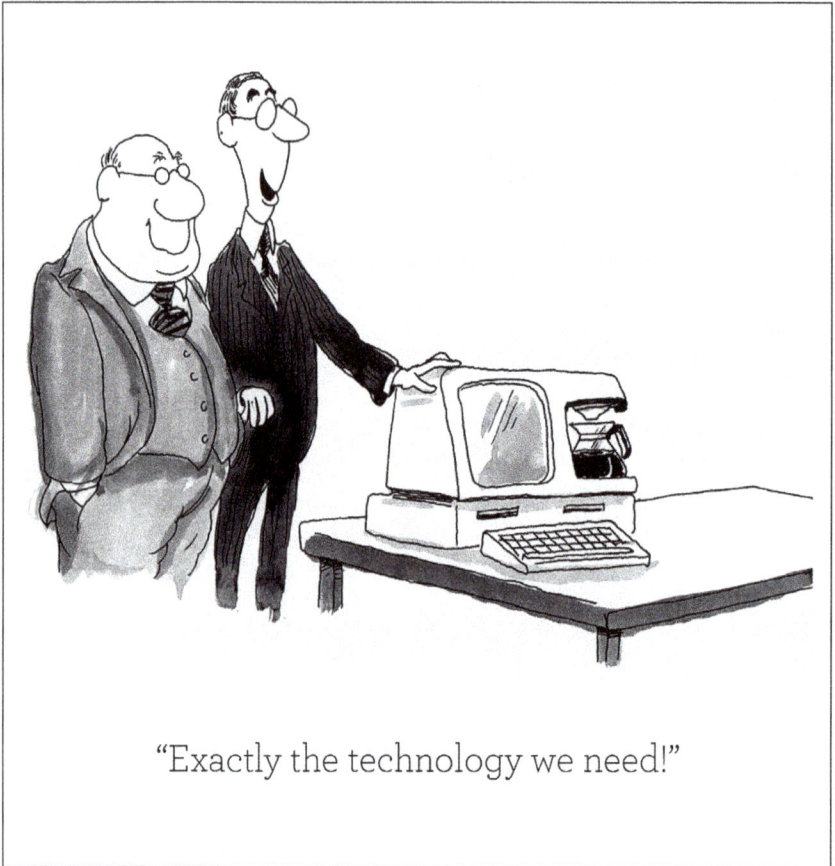

"Exactly the technology we need!"

Share the AHA messages from this book socially by going to
http://aha.pub/5Checks

Section V

Technology Check

Technology is ever-evolving. It just keeps on improving and upgrading as time passes by. Does the technology you have now help you reach your goals? How do you ensure that it's something that can truly help people? With technology, timing is everything. People need to be ready for your technology in order to benefit from it. When building something new or expanding an existing project, ensure that you are using the right technology for the job.

Watch this video: http://aha.pub/5ChecksS5

73

Is your current technology platform going to scale with your business? #MarketingCTO

_____

_____

_____

74

What do we need to put into place in order to make sure this technology can meet its mission? #MarketingCTO

_____

_____

_____

75

How do we upgrade your technology platform? What's working? What needs improvement for long-term viability? #MarketingCTO

_____

_____

_____

76

Do you know where you're going with your technology? If you don't, you'll have a hard time choosing the right solutions. #MarketingCTO

_____

_____

_____

77

Some tech is needlessly complicated.
Ensure the languages and services (stack)
you use are a good fit for the project.
#MarketingCTO

_____

_____

_____

78

Technology is not just about getting things implemented, it's about making sure your users have a great experience. #MarketingCTO

_____

_____

_____

79

Is your tech stack mainstream? Can you find reasonably priced competent developers in abundance to work on your project? #MarketingCTO

_____

_____

_____

80

You don't want to overwhelm people with too many features. Develop for flexibility. #MarketingCTO

_____

_____

_____

81

Create an elegant design so people will be able to find new and innovative things to do with technology you've created. #MarketingCTO

_____

_____

_____

82

You need to understand the resources available. Do you have the right technology in place? Are they available to you?

_____

_____

_____

83

Is your technology at the point where it's commercially viable? #MarketingCTO

_____

_____

_____

84

You can't take your prototype to production.
Be prepared to rebuild. #MarketingCTO

_____

_____

_____

85

Look to see what existing technologies may already be solving the same problem. #MarketingCTO

_____

_____

_____

86

Is there any piece of this that would be a viable commercial product on its own? Spin it off! #MarketingCTO

_____

_____

_____

87

If the idea requires 10 to 100 times more than what you have, leave it in the parking lot for a little while. #MarketingCTO

_____

_____

_____

88

There are some projects that can be done today that probably would not have been viable a few years ago. #MarketingCTO

_____

_____

_____

89

What can we pull off the shelf to get this going? What's available to you in order to make the business viable? #MarketingCTO

_____

_____

_____

90

Ensure that you stay in front of the curve on emerging technologies.
#AI #BlockChain #AR #MarketingCTO

_____

_____

_____

91

Make sure to keep up with the latest innovations so you have choices — not to try to keep up with the Joneses. #MarketingCTO

_____

_____

_____

92

Adopting new technologies is not always a
bad thing. #MarketingCTO

_____

_____

_____

93

To execute your vision, you need to experiment. Play! Dive into technologies that can be used to solve the problem. #MarketingCTO

_____

_____

_____

94

Who is the target market for your project? Is there direct monetization around it? #MarketingCTO

_____

_____

_____

95

Find a financial partner who may want to help you take this to the next level. Crowdsource it? #MarketingCTO

_____

_____

_____

96

Consciously commit to setting up experiments to get the data needed and estimate what happens at scale. #MarketingCTO

_____

_____

_____

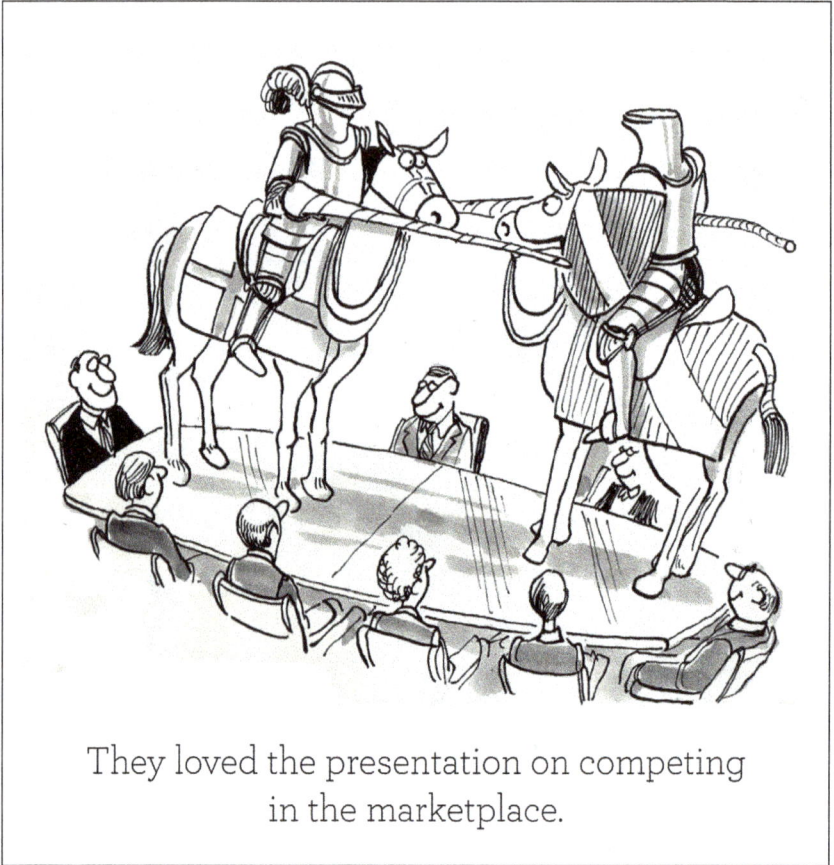

They loved the presentation on competing
in the marketplace.

Share the AHA messages from this book socially by going to
http://aha.pub/5Checks

Section VI

Marketplace Check

The marketplace will determine the success of your project. Ensuring that your target market is ready for your solution and ready to adopt it means that you're also ensuring your project's success. Is there really a marketplace that will pay money for the solution? Are you solving a problem that people actually have, in a way that they will actually adopt? When you get at least ten paying customers, that's when you know you can invest more in the project.

Watch this video: http://aha.pub/5ChecksS6

97

The end goal is to get out a fully featured product that people use to get results. #ResultsMatter #MarketingCTO

_____

_____

_____

98

The money is important, but building products that genuinely solve a problem is fulfilling. #MarketingCTO

_____

_____

_____

99

It's about loving what you do and doing things that make a difference and are in alignment with your overall vision. #MarketingCTO

_____

_____

_____

100

Technology is all about helping your market get the results they want in an easier way. #MarketingCTO

_____

_____

_____

101

Good systems and code allow you to move much faster while retaining stability. #MarketingCTO

_____

_____

_____

102

It's nice when things work as expected and don't blow up. #MarketingCTO

_____

_____

_____

103

These checks only matter in the context of how the product is fulfilling a need in the marketplace. #MarketingCTO

_____

_____

_____

104

Look at all factors, and find out if the solution you're proposing solves a problem in a way people will adopt. #MarketingCTO

_____

_____

_____

105

Don't jump straight into a million-dollar project without knowing if it's going to work in the marketplace. #MarketingCTO

_____

_____

_____

106

The key to product adoption is to create a solution that solves a problem that people actually have. #MarketingCTO

_____

_____

_____

107

You have to be clear on why you're doing something. You have to find out if other people want to use it. #MarketingCTO

_____

_____

_____

108

You and your technology partner are there to solve a problem for people in the marketplace. Are you getting results? #MarketingCTO

_____

_____

_____

109

It really comes down to working with people to help other people. Are you doing that? #MarketingCTO

_____

_____

_____

110

When validating your solution, ensure that not only is the problem solved but also that the market is ready to adopt. #MarketingCTO

_____

_____

_____

"I'm your salesman. I'm your partner."

Share the AHA messages from this book socially by going to
http://aha.pub/5Checks

Section VII

Partner Check

When hiring someone to help you on a project, you need someone you communicate with well. Find a partner, not a vendor or salesperson. A partner is someone you enjoy working with and who has fun working with you. There are other things you can look for when hiring someone. Experience and believability (knowledge and proven track record) can help you determine if a person is a good partner for you. You also need to be able to build trust with your partner. This helps your team and your project be successful. Are you hiring a partner or a vendor?

Watch this video: http://aha.pub/5ChecksS7

111

I'd much rather work with somebody who's there because it's fun and they enjoy it. I'm having fun, are you? #MarketingCTO

_____

_____

_____

112

Work with your team to do fun, fulfilling interesting things, and the sky is the limit. #MarketingCTO

_____

_____

_____

113

If I'm going to hire somebody, I'd much rather hire somebody who's done it before and is good at what they do. #MarketingCTO

_____

_____

_____

114

Hire technology people who understand your commitments and can keep track of the projects on your plate. #MarketingCTO

_____

_____

_____

115

It's fun to work with people who want to play with you vs. people who are there because they feel they have to be. #MarketingCTO

_____

_____

_____

116

If I'm crossing new worlds, I want somebody who's doing the learning with me and enjoys doing it. #MarketingCTO

_____

_____

_____

117

When hiring somebody, ask yourself, "How believable is this person?" #MarketingCTO

_____

_____

_____

118

One of the many factors of believability is experience. Have they done this before? Have they been successful at it? #MarketingCTO

_____

_____

_____

119

If you pay people by the hour, then they'll try to maximize hours worked instead of results obtained. #MarketingCTO

_____

_____

_____

120

Are you comfortable leaving your partner in a room alone with your customer? #MarketingCTO

_____

_____

_____

121

Hire people who work to make a difference and not just to make a paycheck. #MarketingCTO

_____

_____

_____

122

Can your partner be flexible on build vs. buy? "Not invented here" syndrome can kill a project. #MarketingCTO

_____

_____

_____

123

Have somebody who can think through both the marketing side and how to leverage technology to get to that goal. #MarketingCTO

_____

_____

_____

124

Find a partner whom you not only can leave with your customer but whom you can also entrust your prospects and business to.
#MarketingCTO

_____

_____

_____

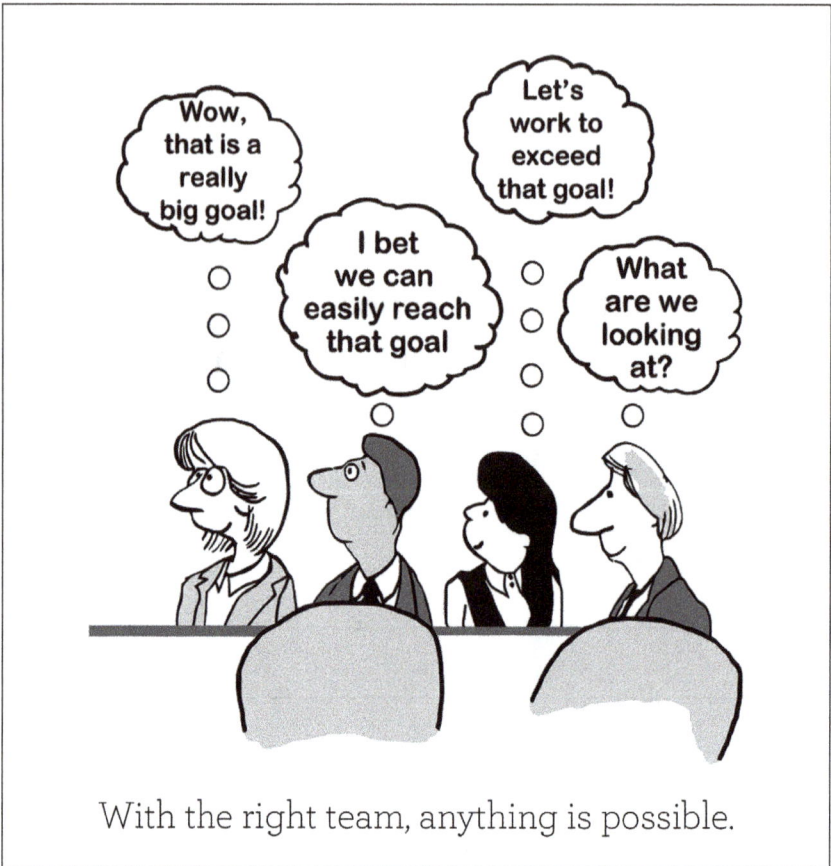

With the right team, anything is possible.

Share the AHA messages from this book socially by going to
http://aha.pub/5Checks

Section VIII

Success through Collaboration

Success and collaboration go hand in hand. When you find a partner whom you collaborate with effectively, success is sure to come. For a project to be successful, you need a partner you trust implicitly. You don't need a lot of people to help you succeed—you just need the right ones. Success through collaboration is sure to come when you have the right partner, the right developers, the right marketer, and the right customers.

Watch this video: http://aha.pub/5ChecksS8

125

Look for a technology partner who is excited to work on this project with you and who knows how to communicate. #MarketingCTO

_____

_____

_____

126

You need a partner whom you trust, so when they say, "No, we should not do that," you believe them implicitly. #MarketingCTO

_____

_____

_____

127

The most important trait of someone you hire is credibility. Are they credible? http://aha.pub/TEDtalk #MarketingCTO

_____

_____

_____

128

If your technology partner doesn't have credibility, it's going to be hard to get investors and others to buy into your vision. #MarketingCTO

129

Work with people who are open and honest about their skills, competencies, and limitations. #MarketingCTO

130

There are many people who were close minded, went with one vendor, and were sold the Kool-Aid. #MarketingCTO

_____

_____

_____

131

There are many good technologies that will solve similar problems in different ways. What should you choose? #MarketingCTO

_____

_____

_____

132

If somebody offers you the world and it sounds too good to be true, it probably is. #MarketingCTO

_____

_____

_____

133

Have somebody who, like you, understands marketing and technology and whom you can have an open honest conversation with. #MarketingCTO

_____

_____

_____

134

It's useful to have a partner to work with on your project; going it alone can be painful in many ways. #MarketingCTO

_____

_____

_____

135

Talking with other knowledgeable people can allow us to trust our gut and move forward with confidence. #MarketingCTO

_____

_____

_____

136

Find a partner who knows how to monetize technology to quickly scale on your experiments and enhance your business. #MarketingCTO

_____

_____

_____

137

There are many people who can build relationships via "know, like, and trust," but are they competent? #MarketingCTO

_____

_____

_____

138

Hire someone not to solve a problem, but because you can collaborate to reach goals, have fun, and make money. #MarketingCTO

_____

_____

_____

139

Hire someone whom you want to grow with and trust implicitly. Are you growing? #MarketingCTO

_____

_____

_____

140

You don't need many people to reach your goals. You just need a handful of the right people. #MarketingCTO

_____

_____

_____

About the Author

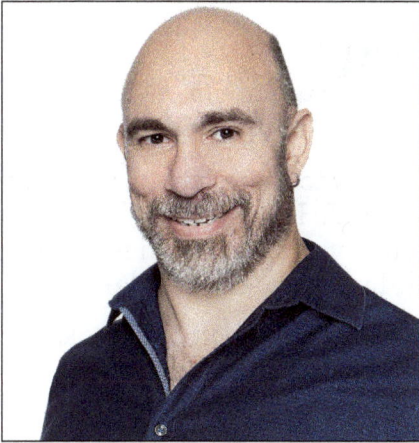

Nick Temple is the founding consultant of Temple Rocks, Inc., a leader in emerging and transformative technologies located in the San Francisco Bay Area/Silicon Valley. Temple offers high-perspective business planning and management, app engineering, integration, and strategic implementation. We specialize in helping people who have working software systems but need to take them to the next level, especially in the field for transformative technologies. Nick is a hands-on software engineer, entrepreneur, and marketer. He is driven by knowing both business systems, as well as technology, and uses his industry experience to help companies and people grow productively and profitability. Nick builds and runs highly scalable systems that have millions of users, as well as helping entrepreneurs bring new ideas from ideation to scale. His company handles projects from ecommerce to gaming and augmented reality, with a focus in the wellness space, including cloud, IoT, desktop, and mobile applications.

AHAthat™

AHAthat makes it easy to share, author, and promote content. There are over 46,000 AHAmessages™ by thought leaders from around the world that you can share in seconds for free on Twitter, Facebook, LinkedIn, and Google+.

For those who want to author their own book, we have a 3-step, time-tested proven process that allows you to write your AHAbook™ of 140 digestible, bite-sized morsels and 5–8 blog posts. Once your content is on AHAthat, you have a customized link that you can use to have your fans/advocates share your content and help you grow your network.

➲ Start sharing: https://AHAthat.com

➲ Start authoring: https://AHAthat.com/Author

Nick Temple
AHAthat Author

Hey, Did You AHAthat™?

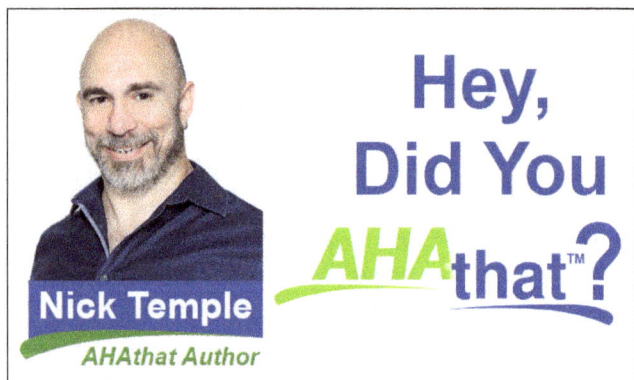

Please go directly to this book in AHAthat and share each AHAmessage socially at
http://aha.pub/5Checks

www.ingramcontent.com/pod-product-compliance
Lightning Source LLC
Chambersburg PA
CBHW071203200326
41519CB00018B/5353